FEARLESS FEMININITY

EMBRACING YOUR POWER UNAPOLOGETICALLY

HAYDE MILLER

ISBN 979-8-218-34960-8
www.iamhaydemiller.com

TABLE OF
CONTENTS

FEARLESS FEMININITY

INTRODUCTION

Welcome, welcome, welcome!

I'm so thrilled you decided to join me on this empowering journey. You know, it's like strapping on a pair of fabulous heels—you're about to walk into a whole new level of fierce.

Now, I know you've got a ton on your plate—life, work, maybe even a sneaky sock-stealing dryer at home. But here you are, making the choice to explore and embrace your own fearless femininity. That's no small feat, and I see you.

So, grab a cozy blanket, a cup of your favorite brew, and let's chat. This isn't just a book; it's a conversation, a sisterhood, a space where we unravel the layers of what it means to be a powerful, fearless woman.

I want you to approach this journey with an open heart, an open mind, and maybe a willingness to dance to your favorite empowering anthem (Beyoncé, anyone?). We're not just turning pages; we're turning corners in our own lives.

Here's the deal: you're about to explore the beauty in your imperfections, find strength you didn't know existed, and fall in love with the extraordinary soul staring back at you in the mirror. It's about time, isn't it?

So, my Queens, get ready to laugh, maybe shed a tear or two, and most importantly, to discover the unstoppable force that is YOU. Because this journey is not just about embracing fearless femininity; it's about celebrating the magic that is uniquely and unapologetically you.

Fearless femininity isn't just a catchphrase; it's a revolution, a declaration, and a celebration of all things uniquely woman.

Now, picture this: Have you ever felt like you're stuck in a box labeled "Society's Expectations"? Girl, we've all been there, trying to fit into molds that weren't made for us. But guess what? That box has nothing on the dynamite that is you. Fearless femininity is saying, "I'll be me, unapologetically, thank you very much!"

In a world that tries to tell us how to walk, talk, and even how much space we should take up, embracing fearless femininity is like sashaying through the world with your own soundtrack playing. Have you ever felt confined by society's expectations? You're not alone, and it's time to break free!

Now, let's talk about those pesky stereotypes—like we're all supposed to be soft-spoken and agreeable. Nah, honey! Fearless femininity is about cranking up the volume on your own opinions, shouting 'em from the rooftops if you need to. We're not here to fit in; we're here to stand out.

This book? It's your guide to smashing those barriers, those labels, and those expectations like the rockstar you are. We're not just turning pages; we're tearing down walls.

—— 99 ——

"A woman is like a tea bag — you
never know
how strong she is
until she gets in hot water."

– Eleanor Roosevelt

———

—— 99 ——

"Life is tough, my darling,
but so are you."

– Stephanie Bennett-Henry

———

—— 99 ——

"Be the type of girl that climbs the
ladder wrong by wrong."

– Mae West

———

Chapter 1
EMBRACING IMPERFECTIONS

Hey Queen,

Welcome to a journey that's all about celebrating the magic in our imperfections! So, let's kick off this fabulous ride with a truth bomb: imperfections aren't roadblocks; they're detours leading to your own kind of perfect.

Now, picture this: Have you ever had a moment when you looked in the mirror and thought, "Girl, what's going on here?" Trust me, we've all been there. But here's the plot twist – those quirks you see? They're not flaws; they're your unique signature, your personal touch on the masterpiece that is you.

I used to be the queen of overthinking about every little "imperfection." My hair? A constant battle. My laugh? Well, it could rival hyenas. But you know what? I've come to realize that these so-called imperfections are what make me shine in a world full of, well, basicness.

Imperfections are like spices in a gumbo—they give flavor to life. Can you imagine a world where everyone looks and acts the same? Boring! It's the quirks, the asymmetry, the uniqueness that make us stand out. So, throw on that crown and sashay down the street, imperfections and all.

Picture young me—a girl with a unique laugh that echoed through the hallways., and a fashion sense that was a bit questionable. But guess what? That distinctive laugh became my trademark. It's the sound of joy, of living life to the fullest. So, next time someone says you're too much or too loud, just remember, girl, you're bringing your own unique soundtrack to this symphony of life.

Oh, and the tears? They flowed like a river. I was a bit on the shy side, navigating the world with a mole by my left eye and a knee that had a rebellious bone sticking out. But here I am today—a published author, flying high as a flight attendant for a major airline, and running my own digital Etsy store.

Imperfections aren't roadblocks; they're steppingstones to greatness. Remember that time I spilled coffee on my job interview outfit? Epic fail, right? But it taught me that life is too short for beige and boring. Now, I rock bold colors like it's my job.

So, Queen, as we dive into this journey together, let's pledge to embrace every freckle, every snort, every twist and turn that makes us beautifully imperfect. Your quirks aren't just details; they're the plot twists in your story. Own them. Celebrate them. And always remember, you're not flawed; you're phenomenal.

You see, some of the fiercest women out there have taken their quirks and turned them into superpowers. Let's take a stroll down Inspiration Avenue.

Oprah Winfrey: Oh, the Queen Mother herself. Did you know she was fired from her first job as a news anchor? Yup, they said she wasn't fit for TV. Fast forward to today, and she's practically the godmother of television, with a net worth that could fund a small country. Lesson learned: setbacks are just setups for major comebacks.

Serena Williams: Now, who could forget the legend that is Serena? People once criticized her body, saying she was too strong for tennis. Can you believe that nonsense? Fast forward again, and she's dominating the court, winning Grand Slam after Grand Slam. She didn't change for anyone; she changed the game.

Tyra Banks: The supermodel who made "smizing" a thing. Back in the day, Tyra was told her forehead was too big. Can you even? Well, guess what? That forehead became a runway for success. She owned it, made it her signature, and now she's running her own empire.

Mindy Kaling: The comedy queen herself. Mindy embraced her Indian heritage and didn't shy away from her body shape. She said, "I'm not going to try to be anything other than who I am," and look at her now—making us laugh and breaking stereotypes.

Rihanna: Bad Gal RiRi! They once told her she was too edgy for the music scene. Edgy? That's like saying water is too wet. She took her uniqueness, wrapped it in confidence, and now she's not just a singer; she's a whole mood.

What do these women have in common? They owned their imperfections, turned criticism into fuel, and walked the runway of life with confidence. They didn't conform; they transformed. So, my Queen, let's take a page from their book. Your quirks are your secret sauce—use them to spice up your story.

It's time to turn that spotlight on you. Yes, you, with all your quirks and charisma. Take a deep breath, grab a mirror, and let's dive into the beauty of embracing your unique imperfections.

Mirror, Mirror on the Wall:
Let's start with a little mirror talk. Have you ever gazed into your reflection and honed in on the so-called "flaws"? Maybe it's a scar, a birthmark, or a feature you've been told isn't 'conventional.' Well, my friend, it's time to flip the script. That scar? It tells a story of resilience. That birthmark? It's your personal piece of art. Let's call them 'beauty marks' because they're uniquely yours.

The Comparison Game:
Now, let's address the comparison game. We've all been down that rabbit hole, scrolling through social media, thinking everyone's got it all figured out. Newsflash: filters and Facetune are not real life. Your journey is unique, and your imperfections are what make it uniquely yours. So, put on those metaphorical blinders and focus on your path.

Rock Your Uniqueness:
What's that one thing about yourself that you've been hesitant to embrace fully? Is it your laughter that can be heard from across the room? Your passion for a hobby that's not 'mainstream'? Whatever it is, it's time to flip the narrative. Your laughter is a melody, and your passions are the colors that make your canvas vibrant.

Embrace the Unconventional:
Let's break free from conventional standards. Embrace the quirks that make you stand out. Your 'imperfections' are like rare diamonds—valuable, cherished, and incomparable.

So, if you've ever thought, "I wish I looked like her" or "I wish I had her confidence," stop right there. You're a limited edition, not a copy.

Celebrate Your Uniqueness:
Take a moment to celebrate the parts of yourself that you've been hiding or downplaying. Whether it's the gap in your teeth, the wild curls, or the snort in your laugh—these are the ingredients that make you a one-of-a-kind masterpiece. Embrace them. Celebrate them. Own them.

So, as you reflect on your own imperfections, remember this: they are not flaws; they are features that add depth and character to your story. Own them like a boss!

Let's dive deep into the trenches of **self-doubt** and **insecurities** because, let's face it, we've all danced with those two troublemakers.

The Self-Doubt Tango
Picture this: a girl, young, ambitious, and filled with dreams. That was me, and maybe that's you too. Self-doubt snuck in like an uninvited guest, whispering, "You're not good enough," "Who do you think you are?" Sound familiar? We've all heard that doubtful tune.

My Inner Critics
I used to have a whole committee of inner critics—think of them as the peanut gallery of negativity. They'd chime in during big moments, saying, "You can't do this" or "Someone else could do it better." But guess what? I didn't kick them out; I made them part of my cheering section. They're like my rowdy cousins now—annoying but kinda endearing.

Defying Expectations

Back in the day, expectations were the weight on my shoulders. People had this idea of who I should be, what I should do. It was like trying to fit into shoes two sizes too small. But breaking free from those expectations? That's when I found my own rhythm, my own groove.

The Rollercoaster of Insecurities

Let's talk insecurities—those rollercoasters of emotions that mess with your mind. Ever felt like you're not smart enough, pretty enough, or just plain enough? Honey, you're not alone. I once had a moment where I questioned every decision, every choice. But guess what? Every stumble was a lesson, every fall a chance to rise.

The Mirror Pep Talk

Imagine standing in front of a mirror, looking yourself in the eyes, and saying, "I am worthy. I am capable. I am more than enough." That mirror pep talk became my daily ritual, and let me tell you, it's a game-changer. Self-love is a muscle, and you gotta flex it regularly.

The Turnaround

Now, the turning point—the moment I realized that doubting myself wasn't protecting me; it was holding me back. So, I flipped the script. Every doubt became a challenge, every insecurity an opportunity to grow. It's like turning lemons into a lemonade stand that sells out every day.

Your turn to share those moments of doubt and insecurity. Let's turn those moments into steppingstones, not stumbling blocks. Remember, every crack in the pavement is a chance for a flower to bloom.

Let's wade in a little deeper with some relatable scenarios, the kind where you might nod your head and think, "Girl, I've been there." Because trust me, we've all navigated those rough seas. Let's sail through some stories that might feel like a page ripped from your own book.

The Impostor Syndrome Shuffle:
Picture this: You're in a room full of accomplished folks, and you start feeling like you snuck in through the back door. Impostor syndrome? Oh, she's an unwelcome guest at many parties. Been there, done that. But you know what I've learned? There's no VIP entrance to success; we all earn our spot.

The Comparison Game Showdown:
Ever scroll through social media, seeing everyone's highlight reels and thinking, "Am I behind in this game called life?" I've had front-row seats to the Comparison Game Showdown, sis. But here's the tea—comparison is a thief of joy. Your journey is your own, and you're exactly where you need to be.

The Perfectly Imperfect Mom Dance:
Let's talk motherhood—the world's toughest gig. Balancing work, kids, and sanity? It's like trying to juggle water balloons. I've had my share of Mom guilt and the infamous "am I doing it right?" moments. Here's a secret: There's no perfect mom; there's just your mom style, and that's exactly what your kids need.

The Relationship Rollercoaster:
Relationships? Oh, honey, they're like rollercoasters—thrilling and terrifying at the same time. From heartbreaks to makeups, I've ridden that emotional rollercoaster. But here's the truth: The right one won't make you feel like you're on a never-ending ride. Love should be a cruise, not a rollercoaster.

The Work-Life Balance Tango:
Trying to balance career ambitions and a personal life? It's like doing the cha-cha on a tightrope. Been there, my friend. But here's a little secret: Balance isn't about doing everything; it's about doing what matters most to you. The rest? It can wait.

The "Am I Enough?" Monologue:
Ever questioned if you're doing enough, being enough? That inner monologue can be louder than a Beyoncé concert. I've had my fair share of self-reflection moments, wondering if I'm measuring up. Spoiler alert: You are more than enough. You're a whole masterpiece.

So, darling, if any of these scenarios hit close to home, know you're not alone. We're all navigating this crazy journey, and every stumble is just a dance move in the rhythm of life.

Here's the thing, sis. The world needs more of you and less of what you think you should be. Authenticity is not about fitting into someone else's mold; it's about proudly being who you are. You're not a copy; you're an original masterpiece.

Ever posted a selfie, only to spend the next hour deciding if it's "Instagram-worthy"? Guilty as charged. But here's a little secret: Those candid moments, the unfiltered laughter, the raw and unedited you—that's the real beauty. Instagram can wait; real life is happening now.

Let's debunk a little myth together. Perfect doesn't exist. It's a mirage, a unicorn we're all chasing. I used to think I had to have it all together, but then I realized life is messy, and that's the beauty of it. Your flaws aren't imperfections; they're the brushstrokes that make your canvas unique.

Your quirks? They're not detours; they're the scenic route of your journey. It's time to own every snort, every goofy dance move, every little thing that makes you, well, you. Forget the script; dance to the beat of your own drum, even if it's a little offbeat.

Imagine a playlist filled with self-love anthems. What would be on yours? Maybe "I'm Every Woman" by Whitney or "Flawless" by Queen Bey? Your self-love anthem is uniquely yours, and it deserves to be played on repeat. You're not just a chapter; you're the whole book.

Remember this: Your flaws don't define you; they make you beautifully unique! Embrace every curve, every scar, every freckle. You're not just a work in progress; you're a masterpiece in motion. Your journey is unfolding, and every step, misstep, and leap forward is part of the dance.

So, put on your crown, stand tall, and let the world see the magic that is you.

Chapter 2
UNLEASHING INNER STRENGTH

Now, let's dive into a topic that's like finding money in last winter's coat pocket—unleashing the untapped potential within every one of us. I'm talking about that powerhouse of strength, resilience, and magic that's just waiting to be discovered.

Girl, You Got It: Ever felt like there's this untapped well of potential within you? Like you're sitting on a treasure chest, but the key is playing hide-and-seek? Well, sis, let me tell you, that potential is in there, just itching to break free. It's the secret sauce to your greatness.

No More Playing Small: Why do we often shrink ourselves, like we're trying to fit into a pair of jeans after Thanksgiving dinner? Newsflash: Your potential doesn't have a size limit. It's expansive, boundless, and refuses to be confined. So, let's stop playing small and start embracing the vastness of what we're truly capable of.

The Treasure Hunt Begins: Imagine your untapped potential as a treasure map, and you're the daring explorer. It's time to grab that compass and navigate the uncharted territories within you. What talents, skills, or passions have been patiently waiting for their spotlight? Let's dust them off and let them shine.

The Power of Resilience: Life throws curveballs, hurricanes, and sometimes a whole kitchen sink at us. But here's the thing—your untapped potential is like a superhero cape. It's your resilience, your ability to bounce back stronger and wiser. Remember, the strongest trees weather the fiercest storms.

Your Magic Wand: You, my friend, have a magic wand disguised as untapped potential. It's the tool that turns dreams into reality, obstacles into steppingstones, and challenges into triumphs. Don't underestimate the power of your own magic.

Unlocking Your Inner Superhero: Here's the tea: Your untapped potential is the key to unlocking your inner superhero. Whether you're conquering career goals, navigating personal challenges, or simply finding joy in the everyday, that potential is your sidekick, cheering you on.

Your greatness awaits, and trust me, it's ready to shine brighter than a diamond.

And what's the key to unlocking this powerhouse? Well, grab your magnifying glass because we're introducing exercises that'll have you discovering your passions and strengths in no time.

Passion Quest: Imagine this exercise as your personal treasure hunt, but instead of X marking the spot, it's your heart. What gets your heart racing? What makes time fly because you're so engrossed? Whether it's belting out tunes in the shower or organizing your sock drawer like a pro, your passions are the breadcrumbs leading to your untapped potential.

Strength Safari: Now, close your eyes (not if you're driving, please) and picture yourself as a safari explorer. Your strengths are the majestic animals roaming freely in your personal wildlife reserve. What are you naturally good at? What makes you feel invincible? Grab your mental binoculars, and let's spot those strengths from a mile away.

Passion Planner: Okay, let's get a bit more practical. It's time to dust off that planner (or open the app—no judgment here). Schedule some quality time with your passions. Whether it's a weekly painting session or a monthly stargazing date, make a commitment to do what you love. Trust me; your passions will thank you with bursts of inspiration and joy.

Strength Selfie: Now, let's take a selfie—a strength selfie, that is. Jot down three strengths that you know deep down make you a rockstar. Don't be shy; this is your moment to shine. Post that strength selfie somewhere you'll see it daily, like a virtual sticky note for your soul.

Passion Playlist: Lastly, what's a good exercise without a killer playlist? Create a playlist that resonates with your passions. Whether it's the soulful beats of R&B or the empowering anthems of pop, let the music be the soundtrack to your passion-fueled journey.

Your passions and strengths are like the superhero cape you never knew you had.

Let's dive into a truth bomb—I need you to know that your strength is limitless, Diva! Yup, you heard it right. We're not talking about that "lift a car with one finger" kind of strength (although, hey, if you can do that, major kudos), but the kind that moves mountains, shakes the ground, and takes charge of your own narrative.

Imagine your strength as a bottomless bag of glitter. No matter how much you sprinkle around, there's always more. Your strength isn't confined to a set amount or a specific moment; it's a dazzling, never-ending reservoir waiting for you to tap into.

Grab my hand, and let's unlock that strength together. It's like having a secret handshake with your superhero self. Picture us standing side by side, capes billowing in the wind, ready to conquer whatever comes our way. Your strength is the key, and we're turning that lock together.

I want you to repeat after me, "My strength is limitless, and I am a force to be reckoned with!" Say it loud, say it proud. Your strength isn't shy or timid; it's bold, unapologetic, and ready to take center stage. You're not just a player in the game; you're the headliner.

Your strength is like a fine wine; it gets better with time, and, darling, you're just getting started.

Let's do a little strength treasure hunting, shall we? Picture this as a quest to unveil the incredible powerhouse that's been hanging out within you. I promise, it's like discovering a secret stash of joy in the back of your closet—exciting and oh-so necessary. Get your pens ready, because we're about to spill some ink and uncover the strength within.

The Gratitude Journal: Start by acknowledging the strengths you already possess. Each day, jot down three things you're grateful for about yourself. It could be your kindness, your wit, or your tenacity. These daily affirmations are like vitamins for your self-esteem.

Passion Time: Now, let's dive into your passion pit. What makes your heart race? What activity feels less like work and more like a party you never want to leave? Whether it's painting, salsa dancing, or perfecting your grandma's secret pancake recipe, that passion holds the key to your strength.

Superpower Moments: Reflect on your life's superhero moments. Think back to times when you faced challenges and came out on top. What were you doing? What strengths did you unleash to conquer the hurdles? Your superhero moments are like breadcrumbs leading to your inner strength goldmine.

Survey Says: Let's play a little game of Strength Family Feud. Reach out to friends, family, or that one person who owes you a favor (we all have one) and ask them what strengths they see in you. It's like getting the audience's perspective on your own game show of fabulousness.

Dream Vision Board: Grab some magazines, a glue stick, and unleash your inner artist. Create a vision board filled with images and words that resonate with your dream self—the strong, fearless, unstoppable you. It's like a visual love letter to your inner strength.

Strength Mantra: Lastly, let's craft your own strength mantra. It's like a personal power anthem you can recite whenever you need a boost. Think of a phrase that makes you feel invincible, like "I am resilient," or "My strength knows no bounds."

How did it feel to uncover these aspects of yourself? What surprised you the most? This reflection is like a snapshot of your strength evolution, and trust me, it's a journey worth revisiting.

Ever hear that saying, "The only limit is the one you set yourself"? Well, it's true, and you, my friend, are the CEO of breaking through those self-set limits. You've got the keys to your own powerhouse, and guess what? It's time to throw open those doors and let that strength flood out like sunshine after a storm.

Think of your inner strength like a secret sauce—a magical blend of resilience, courage, and a dash of fabulousness. You can conquer any challenge that comes your way. Seriously, if challenges had a "Do Not Disturb" sign, they'd put it up when they see you coming.

So, here's the deal—I want you to repeat after me: "I am a force to be reckoned with, and I am ready to unleash that power!" It's not just a mantra; it's a declaration. Your power isn't meant to be stored away like those shoes you only wear on special occasions. No, honey, it's time to take them off the shelf and strut like you own the runway.

You've faced challenges before, right? Maybe you conquered a mountain or two, or perhaps you faced a dragon and lived to tell the tale. Well, guess what? Those challenges didn't break you; they made you the unstoppable force you are today. And the best part? There's more strength where that came from.

Chapter 3
AUTHENTICITY AND SELF-LOVE

Now, I know we're living in a world that sometimes feels like it's handing out scripts on how we should act, talk, and even slay. But guess what? The only script you need is the one written by the fabulous author that is YOU.

Raise your hand if you've ever scrolled through social media, comparing your backstage to someone else's highlight reel. Yep, me too. We're bombarded with images of perfect lives, flawless faces, and curated moments that make us question our own fabulousness. But, sis, let me tell you, those snapshots don't tell the whole story.

Imagine if we all looked and acted the same. How boring would that be? Your quirks, your unique laugh, the way you snort when you're laughing too hard—those are the things that make you authentically YOU. Don't trade them in for a cookie-cutter version of someone else.

Society loves to hand out expectations like Oprah giving away cars. But here's the thing, Queen: you don't need to conform to anyone else's idea of perfection. It's time for a detox, a cleanse of societal expectations. Throw that pressure to conform out the window and let your authenticity shine through like a disco ball at a '70s party.

Authenticity is like the secret sauce to self-love. It's embracing the real you, flaws and all. So, let's do a little exercise. Look in the mirror and say, "I love the real me." Go ahead, say it. Doesn't that feel like a warm hug for your soul?

Think of authenticity as your secret superpower. It's the force that connects you to others, the magnetism that draws people in. When you embrace your true self, you create a space for others to do the same. You become a trendsetter in a world full of followers.

Let's make a pact to ditch the comparison game. Your journey is uniquely yours, and there's no need to measure up to someone else's yardstick. Comparison is like trying to fit a round peg into a square hole—impossible and utterly unnecessary.

Let's celebrate the authentic you. Your quirks, your laugh, your style—they're not just parts of you; they're the masterpiece that is YOU. And remember, in a world that sometimes feels like it's asking you to be someone else, your authenticity is your rebellion, your protest, and your triumph.

Here's a mantra that should be on your lips every single day: "I am enough, just as I am!" Now, I know, I know, it's easier said than done, but trust me, it's a declaration we all need to rock like our favorite pair of stilettos.

Slaying the "Not Enough" Dragon: Ever feel like there's a little dragon on your shoulder whispering, "You're not enough, girl"? Well, it's time to grab that dragon by its fiery tail and toss it out the window. Because, honey, you are more than enough just as you are.

The Perfection Trap: Society has this sneaky way of making us feel like we're in a never-ending audition for a role that doesn't exist. Perfect hair, perfect body, perfect life—what is this, a fairy tale? Let's break that illusion and say, "I am enough, imperfections and all."

Comparison, Be Gone: Comparison is the thief of joy, and we're not letting it steal one more moment. Your journey is uniquely yours, like a signature scent that lingers in a room. So, let's toss the comparison game out the window and declare, "I am enough, just as I am."

Your Unique Recipe: Think of yourself as a recipe—extra spicy, with a dash of sass and a whole lot of fabulousness. It's time to stop looking at other people's recipes and embrace your own flavor. You're not missing any ingredients; you're the perfect blend.

Self-Love Swagger: Self-love isn't just a hashtag; it's a swagger, a strut, a celebration of the amazing being that is YOU. So, let's stand in front of that mirror, hairbrush microphone in hand, and belt out, "I am enough, and I'm owning it!"

Rock Your Crown: You, my Queen, wear an invisible crown. It's not about being a flawless monarch; it's about owning your queendom, flaws and all. So, lift that crown a little higher and declare, "I am enough, and my queendom is fabulous."

Unleash Your Magic: Remember, you're not a work in progress waiting for perfection to sprinkle down like fairy dust. You're a masterpiece in motion, a canvas painted with every laugh, every tear, and every triumph. So, let's unleash that magic and proudly say, "I am enough, just as I am!"

So, my beautiful beings, let this be your anthem, your battle cry, and your daily affirmation. You're not striving for perfection; you're reveling in your perfectly imperfect self. And to that, we say, "I am enough, just as I am."

Let's chat about something that's as unique as grandma's secret gumbo recipe—your quirks and idiosyncrasies. You know, those little personality gems that make you stand out in a crowd.

Picture life as a spice bazaar, and your quirks are the rare, exotic flavors that everyone secretly wants to try but might be too afraid to. Are you the one who laughs a little too loud? Perfect! Are you a dancing machine in your living room? Fantastic! Your quirks are what make this flavor-packed journey called life so darn delicious.

Think of your quirks like a symphony of uniqueness. Each quirk plays its own instrument, creating a melody that's exclusively yours. So, let that laugh be the trumpet announcing your arrival and that dance move be the drumroll of your awesomeness.

Quirkology—it's a real thing! Your quirks are like brushstrokes on the canvas of your personality. They're the little details that turn a regular painting into a masterpiece. Embrace those quirks like an artist embraces every stroke, creating a portrait that captivates and inspires.

Newsflash, Queen: You're not supposed to fit into a one-size-fits-all mold. Your quirks aren't accidental; they're intentional brushstrokes of your fabulous self. So, let's celebrate the fact that you're not a copy; you're an original, a limited edition, a one-and-only masterpiece.

Remember those times you tried to dim your quirks to fit in? Well, no more of that nonsense! Your quirks are your secret power play. They're the unexpected twist in the plot, the surprise ending that leaves everyone in awe. So, let's embrace the quirk power play and declare, "I am uniquely fabulous, quirks and all!"

Consider your quirks the VIP pass to the exclusive Quirk Club. It's a gathering of the most interesting, fascinating people—the ones who embrace their quirks like badges of honor. So, grab your membership card and join the club, because normal is overrated, and quirks are where the real party's at.

Here's a challenge for you, my lovely friends: Embrace one of your quirks today. Maybe it's that snort when you laugh or that dance move you reserve for solo dance-offs. Whatever it is, let it shine. Your quirks aren't just quirks; they're the crown jewels in your authenticity.

So, my quirktastic Queens, wear your quirks like a tiara. Let them be the crowning glory of your fabulous self. Because when you embrace your quirks, you're not just living; you're living authentically, and that's a beautiful thing.

Pull up a chair, because I've got some tales that'll have you embracing your quirks with a big ol' smile.

The Laugh That Led to Love: Picture this: a crowded plane, two strangers seated next to each other, and a contagious laugh that echoed through the cabin. Little did she know, Jenna's infectious laughter caught the attention of a fellow passenger—her future husband. He couldn't help but be drawn to the joy radiating from that row. Fast forward to today, and they share a life filled with love and laughter, all because Jenna embraced her unmistakable, snort-induced giggles.

27

The Dance Floor Entrepreneur: Meet Mariah, the queen of unconventional dance moves. At every party, she would break out into a dance style that was uniquely hers. One day, a filmmaker spotted her on the dance floor and was captivated by her carefree moves. Next thing you know, Mariah found herself in the spotlight, starring in a dance-themed movie that celebrated authenticity and uniqueness. Her quirk became her signature, opening doors to a career she had never imagined.

Mismatched Shoes, Match Made in Heaven: In a sea of fashion conformity, enter Alex, a young woman known for her bold fashion choices. One day, she accidentally walked into a high-profile event wearing mismatched shoes. Instead of hiding, she confidently strutted through the room. Surprisingly, a fashion designer in attendance was inspired by her fearless approach to style. They collaborated on a collection that celebrated embracing imperfections, turning Alex's fashion faux pas into a trendsetting statement.

The Office Snort: In the corporate jungle, where seriousness often reigns, enter Jake, the guy with the unmistakable snort when he finds something hilariously funny. During a tense presentation, Jake's snort unintentionally echoed through the silent room. Rather than embarrassment, his authentic reaction broke the tension and brought a moment of much-needed levity. The team began to appreciate Jake's ability to infuse humor into serious situations, ultimately improving team morale and productivity.

The Kitchen Catastrophe Chef: Chef Olivia had a reputation for her experimental cooking disasters. One day, she mistakenly combined unexpected ingredients in a dish, creating a flavor explosion that stunned her dinner guests. The surprising success landed her a cooking show where she continued to embrace her unconventional culinary style.

Olivia's quirky kitchen catastrophes became the secret ingredient to her culinary success.

So, my vibrant Queens, let these stories be a reminder that your quirks aren't just unique to you; they can be the unexpected steppingstones to joy, love, and success. Embrace them like confetti at a celebration because, in the grand story of life, your quirks are the sparkles that make it truly magical.

Picture your life as a symphony, and every quirk, every laugh, every dance move is a unique note in your composition. It's not about playing someone else's sheet music; it's about creating your own melody. Your quirks aren't wrong notes; they're the crescendo that makes your symphony uniquely yours.

Stand tall, twirl in the spotlight, and let your quirks take center stage. Your laughter is a note of joy, your dance moves are the rhythm of your soul, and your uniqueness is the melody that makes the whole world tap their feet.

In a world that sometimes feels like it hands out critiques instead of applause, self-love is your standing ovation. It's not about perfection; it's about embracing the perfectly imperfect you. So, stand in front of that mirror, look yourself in the eyes, and say, "I love you, quirks and all." Your reflection is a masterpiece in progress, and the artist is none other than you.

Queen, your uniqueness isn't a flaw to be fixed; it's a superpower to be celebrated. It's the secret sauce, the magic wand, the glitter that sets you apart. Your quirks aren't a liability; they're an asset, a currency of authenticity in a world that sometimes deals in conformity. So, wear your quirks like a crown, and let them be the jewels in your self-love kingdom.

Chapter 4
BUILDING CONFIDENCE

Now, I don't want you to just walk; I want you to strut, and we're going to make sure that crown on your head is sitting just right. So, grab your favorite mirror, and let's talk about boosting that confidence in every area of your fabulous life.

Mirror Pep Talk: First things first, let's start with the morning ritual—the mirror pep talk. I want you to look yourself square in the eyes and say, "I am a force to be reckoned with!" You're not just getting ready; you're gearing up to conquer the day. Remember, confidence starts with the first conversation you have every morning, and that's the one with yourself.

Power Pose Magic: Ever heard of power posing? It's not just for superheroes; it's for queens like you too. Strike a power pose before a big meeting or a significant event. Stand tall, shoulders back, chin up. It's like a mini coronation ceremony where you declare, "I am here, and I am powerful!" Your body language sends signals to your brain, and trust me, it works like a charm.

Affirmation Magic: Let's talk affirmations. Now, I'm not saying you need to be in front of the mirror reciting Shakespearean soliloquies, but a good dose of positive affirmations can do wonders. Repeat after me, "I am confident, capable, and absolutely fabulous!" Your words have power, and when you affirm your greatness, you're creating a confidence manifesto that echoes through your day.

Dress for Success: Clothes aren't just fabric; they're your armor of confidence. Wear outfits that make you feel like you could conquer a kingdom. Whether it's power heels, a bold lipstick, or your lucky earrings, let your attire be a reminder of the queen that you are. Remember, when you look good, you feel good, and when you feel good, confidence follows like your shadow.

Learn, Grow, Slay: Confidence isn't about having all the answers; it's about knowing you can figure it out. So, be a lifelong learner. Whether it's a new skill, a hobby, or mastering the art of perfectly flipping a pancake, embrace the process of learning. The more you know, the more you grow, and the more you grow, the more you slay. It's a confidence evolution, and you're at the helm.

Embrace Your Uniqueness: Here's a little secret: confidence is like a fingerprint—unique to each person. Embrace the things that make you stand out. Whether it's your quirky laugh, your distinctive sense of humor, or the fact that you can recite every line from your favorite movie, let those quirks be the jewels in your confidence crown. Remember, you're not meant to fit in; you're meant to stand out.

Confidence isn't a one-size-fits-all; it's a bespoke gown tailored just for you.

Imagine your confidence as a red carpet, and imposter syndrome? Well, it's not on the guest list. Confidence is about recognizing your achievements, big or small, and owning them. So, let's roll out that red carpet, sprinkle some confidence, and make every step you take a strut of triumph.

Take a moment, grab your favorite notebook, and jot down your achievements. Big wins, small victories—they all count. Sometimes, we forget just how amazing we are. Your achievements are your resume of resilience, your proof that you're not an imposter but a conqueror.

Remember, the comparison trap is the VIP lounge for imposter syndrome. We see others succeed, and suddenly, we question our own journey. Let me tell you something, Queen: everyone's journey is different, and your path is uniquely yours. Instead of comparing, celebrate. Your success doesn't diminish anyone else's; it amplifies the collective power of Queens ruling the world.

So, here's our mantra for today: "Imposter syndrome, you're not welcome here. I am the author of my story, the captain of my ship, and I am owning every step of this journey." Repeat it like a battle cry, because we're not just kicking imposter syndrome to the curb; we're sending it packing.

Take a selfie, strike a power pose, and caption it with one word that describes your confidence. Share it with someone you trust, because your confidence journey is a shared celebration.

Let's kick that unwanted guest to the curb and make room for the true star—your unapologetic, confident self.

Now that we've shown that imposter syndrome the door, let's roll up our sleeves and get into the nitty-gritty of building that unshakable confidence. We're not talking about overnight transformations; we're talking about gradual, steady growth—the kind that feels like a cozy blanket, warming you up to your own greatness.

Think of building confidence like a workout routine. We're not going from zero to a hundred in a single session; we're sculpting those confidence muscles over time.

Like I said earlier, start with the small victories. Did you rock a meeting today? Celebrate it! Did you conquer a fear? High five yourself! We often overlook the small wins, but they're the building blocks of big successes. Your journey is made up of these triumphs, so celebrate them like you're popping the champagne at your own success party.

Remember those quirks we celebrated earlier? It's time to turn them into confidence boosters. Take a moment to jot down three things that make you uniquely you. Maybe it's your infectious laugh, your impressive dance moves, or your ability to make a killer cup of coffee. Own these quirks; they're your secret weapons in the confidence arsenal.

Close your eyes and visualize your most confident self. Picture the way you walk, the way you talk, the energy you exude. Now, step into that visualization. Imagine wearing your confidence like a tailored suit or a stunning gown. Visualization is a powerful tool to make your future self your present reality.

Confidence is a journey of expansion. Identify one thing slightly outside your comfort zone and take a step towards it. It could be speaking up in a meeting, trying a new activity, or networking with someone new. Stretching your comfort zone is like giving your confidence muscles a good workout—they'll thank you for it.

Create a confidence journal. Reflect on your wins, your affirmations, and the steps you're taking outside your comfort zone. Journaling is like capturing the essence of your confidence journey. It's a tangible reminder of your growth and flipping through those pages will be like revisiting the highlights of your confidence story.

Let's treat building confidence like a journey—a journey filled with laughter, self-discovery, and the empowering realization that every small step is a stride towards the confident Queen you're becoming.

It's time to sprinkle in some magic—affirmation magic! Picture them as your personal cheerleaders, hyping you up in every situation. So, grab your affirmation pom-poms, and let's create a list that'll have you walking on sunshine, no matter the weather.

Affirmations are like your personal power playlist. They're not just words; they're the beats that set the rhythm of your confidence dance. We're going to tailor these affirmations to different situations, like a wardrobe of words that suits every occasion.

Facing a Challenge: When you're gearing up to conquer a challenge, your affirmation should be your battle cry. Something like, "I am strong, capable, and ready for any challenge that comes my way!" Picture this affirmation as your armor, shielding you from self-doubt and hesitation.

Stepping Outside Your Comfort Zone: For those moments when you're about to take a leap outside your comfort zone, your affirmation should be like a trampoline that propels you forward. How about, "I am courageous, and with every step, I'm expanding my horizons!" Let this affirmation be the wind beneath your wings, lifting you to new heights.

Embracing Your Uniqueness: When it's time to celebrate your quirks and uniqueness, your affirmation should be a love letter to yourself. Try something like, "I embrace my quirks; they make me beautifully unique. I am a masterpiece in progress!" Let this affirmation be your love anthem, playing on repeat.

Dealing with Setbacks: In the face of setbacks, your affirmation should be your comeback anthem. How about, "I am resilient. Every setback is a setup for a greater comeback!" Let this affirmation be your bounce-back soundtrack, turning setbacks into steppingstones.

Navigating Uncertainty: When sailing through the sea of uncertainty, your affirmation should be your guiding star. Try, "I trust in the journey, even when the path is unclear. I am the captain of my ship!" Let this affirmation be your compass, steering you confidently through the unknown.

Daily Confidence Boost: And for your daily dose of confidence, your affirmation should be like a morning espresso—a quick pick-me-up. Something like, "I am confident, capable, and absolutely fabulous!" Let this affirmation be the kickstart to your day, setting the tone for confidence greatness.

Choose one affirmation for each situation and say them out loud daily. Bonus points for saying them in front of the mirror, channeling your inner confidence superstar. Trust me; your reflection will thank you. Let's create a symphony of empowering words that'll be the soundtrack to your confidence journey.

Now that we've decked out our affirmation wardrobe, it's time to turn up the volume and let your confidence anthem blast through the speakers. Imagine this as your personal concert, and you're the headlining act. So, grab your microphone (or hairbrush, I won't judge), and let's belt out the affirmations like we're hitting the high notes of self-love.

The Confidence Anthem: Picture this: You, standing in front of a mirror, ready to launch your personal confidence concert. The spotlight is on you, and the crowd is cheering. Now, let's kick off this anthem with a motivational mantra: "Repeat after me, 'I am confident, I am powerful, I am unstoppable!'"

Verse 1: Let's start with the basics. Stand tall, shoulders back, and repeat after me: "I am confident." Feel it in your bones, let it resonate in your voice. Confidence isn't just a feeling; it's a declaration, and you're proclaiming it to the universe.

Chorus: Now, let's move to the power section. Repeat with authority: "I am powerful." Imagine each word sending ripples of power through your being. You're not asking for power; you're declaring it, and the universe is taking notes.

Verse 2: Here comes the unstoppable force verse. With unwavering determination, say it loud: "I am unstoppable!" Imagine obstacles crumbling in the face of your unstoppable energy. This isn't wishful thinking; it's a statement of fact.

Bridge: Now, let's build to a crescendo. Repeat the entire mantra like you're reaching the climax of a soul-stirring ballad: "I am confident, I am powerful, I am unstoppable!" Feel the energy surge through you, like the beat of a bass drum propelling you forward.

Repeat the Encore: But wait, we're not done yet. In the world of confidence anthems, encores are a must. Repeat the mantra, add your own variations, dance a little if you feel like it. This is your show, and you're stealing the spotlight.

Confidence Jam Session: Now, turn up the volume on your favorite confidence-boosting song. Dance, sing, let the music elevate your spirits. You're not just a listener; you're the DJ of your confidence journey.

Confidence Anthem Challenge: Challenge yourself to have a daily confidence anthem session. Play your favorite song, repeat your mantra, and let the positive vibes linger. Soon, you'll find that your confidence anthem is more than just words; it's a melody that resonates with your soul.

Let's hit those high notes, own the stage, and make your confidence anthem the chart-topper of your life.

Chapter 5
NAVIGATING CHALLENGES

Let's talk about challenges. We've all faced them; they're like those unexpected guests who show up uninvited. But here's the twist: challenges, my dear, are not roadblocks; they're opportunities to flex your resilience muscles.

Let's look at some tales of resilience—stories of challenges faced by some remarkable women. Life handed them lemons, but oh, did they make the sweetest lemonade.

- Meet Sarah, our career queen. She hit a snag in her dream job —a promotion she'd worked hard for slipped through her fingers. It was a moment of setback and disappointment, a roadblock in her professional climb.

- Jasmine, the queen of relationship resilience, found herself in the midst of a heartbreak. A relationship that seemed like forever crumbled, leaving her feeling like a mosaic of shattered emotions.

- Rachel, the dreamer with big business dreams, faced a daunting dragon—financial hurdles that threatened to thwart her entrepreneurial journey. It seemed like the universe had a strict price for chasing dreams.

- And then there's Maya, the resilient mom who danced the juggling act of balancing career, family, and personal dreams. Each day felt like a challenge of its own, a chaotic puzzle to solve.

Now, take a moment to reflect on the challenges you've faced. Challenges aren't roadblocks; they're invitations to grow. Every setback is a setup for a comeback, and you, my dear, are the author of your story.

Let's check in on our sisters and see how heroines arose from the challenges they faced.

Remember Sarah, the career climber? Well, after that promotion setback, she didn't throw in the towel. Nope, not our Sarah. She turned that disappointment into motivation, enrolled in skill-boosting courses, networked like a pro, and guess what? The next opportunity that knocked on her door found her not just ready but supercharged. Sarah turned a setback into a steppingstone for a career leap.

After her setback, she didn't just bounce back; she soared higher. The lesson here? Every setback is a setup for a comeback. So, to all my Queens out there facing a career curveball, remember, setbacks are just detours on the road to success. Embrace the journey; the view from the top is worth it.

Now, let's check in on Jasmine, the relationship re-setter. Heartbreak is no joke, but Jasmine didn't let it define her. Through therapy, self-love rituals (picture her with a face mask, cueing the self-love playlist), and a dash of humor, she emerged stronger. Jasmine learned that challenges could be catalysts for self-discovery and growth. She turned her heartbreak into a breakthrough.

The takeaway? You are not the sum of your heartbreaks; you're the sum of your heart's triumphs. So, Queens in matters of love, let your heartbreaks be the steppingstones to self-love. The best chapters are yet to be written.

Rachel, our dream entrepreneur facing a financial dragon, didn't back down. She got creative, started a side hustle, and navigated the financial maze. It wasn't easy, but Rachel's determination turned financial hurdles into a launchpad for innovation. Today, she's not just chasing dreams; she's catching them.

Rachel didn't let a tight budget dim her dreams; she turned it into a launchpad for innovation. The message? Dreams don't come with a price tag; they come with determination. So, my dream-chasing Queens, let your creativity be your currency. The dream is yours for the taking.

Last but not least, let's swing by Maya, the resilient mom mastering the juggling act. Maya embraced the chaos, learned the art of delegation (probably with superhero-level organizational skills), and celebrated the imperfectly perfect moments. She discovered that challenges weren't roadblocks; they were messy ingredients in life's recipe. Maya turned chaos into a symphony of joy.

Maya danced through chaos and found joy in the imperfectly perfect moments. The revelation? Life's messy moments are the spices that make it flavorful. So, to my Queens juggling a million things, let each juggle be a dance, and celebrate the chaos; it's your unique rhythm.

The stories of Sarah, Jasmine, Rachel, and Maya aren't just tales; they're lessons in resilience, determination, and the magic of turning challenges into victories.

These women faced it all and triumphed; so can you, Queen! Challenges are not stop signs; they're speed bumps on the road of life. Triumph isn't reserved for a select few; it's a crown waiting for every Queen who dares to face challenges head-on.

Let's explore a few more challenges that many women might encounter, both personally and professionally, and the practical strategies to not just face setbacks but to turn them into your personal runway for success.

The Professional Pivot Predicament: Ever find yourself at a career crossroads, unsure which way to go? It's like standing at a buffet and not knowing which dish will satisfy your professional hunger. Take a breath, Queen. This is not a roadblock; it's a chance to explore new flavors. The strategy? Sample a bit of everything. Attend workshops, network like a pro, and soon you'll find your professional feast.

The Relationship Rollercoaster: Relationships, ah, the rollercoaster of emotions. Sometimes the ride feels bumpy, and you're wondering if you accidentally stepped on the wrong coaster. Fear not, Queen. This isn't a derailment; it's a reroute to love. Strategy time? Buckle up and communicate. Share your feelings, listen, and remember that love's journey is full of unexpected turns.

The Budget Blues: Financial woes hitting you like an unexpected bill in the mail? It happens to the best of us. But here's the plot twist—it's not a dead-end street; it's a detour to financial finesse. Strategy in action? Budget like a boss. Track your expenses, cut back on non-essentials, and watch how your financial story takes a turn for the better.

The Time Tango Trouble: Feeling like you're in a dance-off with time and it's winning? Sister, it's not a defeat; it's a chance to choreograph your own routine. Strategy spotlight? Prioritize like a pro. Identify what truly matters, delegate tasks, and watch how your time management skills become the dance moves everyone wants to copy.

The Self-Care Struggle: Balancing work, family, and personal time can make self-care seem like a luxury rather than a necessity. Transform this challenge into a priority by scheduling dedicated self-care time. Treat it as non-negotiable, whether it's a bubble bath, a good book, or a nature walk.

The Decision Dilemma: Making significant life decisions can be paralyzing, leading to a fear of making the wrong choice. Turn this challenge into a decision-making superpower by breaking down choices into smaller, manageable steps. Seek advice, weigh pros and cons, and remember that decisions are opportunities for growth.

The Work-Life Balance Waltz: Juggling the demands of a career and personal life can feel like a constant dance, leaving little room for rest. Turn this challenge into a well-choreographed routine by setting clear boundaries. Define specific work hours, schedule family time, and make time for hobbies. Remember, balance is about harmony, not perfection.

The Networking Nudge: Networking events can feel like navigating uncharted social territories, making it challenging to connect with others. Turn this challenge into an opportunity by adopting a mindset of curiosity. Ask open-ended questions, share your story, and remember, networking is about building relationships, not collecting business cards.

The Confidence Conundrum: Many women face imposter syndrome or self-doubt, questioning whether they're truly qualified or deserving of their achievements. Flip the script by embracing your accomplishments. Keep a success journal, document positive feedback, and surround yourself with a support system that reminds you of your worth.

Life, my Queens, is like a GPS that sometimes takes you on unexpected routes. Challenges? They're like those detours. They might make you take a few extra turns, but trust me, you're still on the road to greatness. So, the next time life throws you a curveball, remember, challenges are just scenic routes, not dead ends.

Challenges are universal, and we're in this sisterhood of triumph together. Imagine us with our GPS navigating through the twists and turns, laughing, singing, and maybe even taking a dance break. Because challenges don't stand a chance when faced with a sisterhood like ours.

If life had a playlist, setbacks would be just the interludes between the power anthems of triumph. So, crank up that volume, put on your invisible crown, and dance through the challenges. You're not alone, you are part of a resilient squad that turns setbacks into setups for epic comebacks.

Remember that challenges are not roadblocks; they're invitations to grow, learn, and become even more fabulous. So, my resilient Queens, wear your setbacks like badges of honor. You're not just navigating challenges; you're conquering them with style and grace.

Chapter 6
SETTING BOUNDARIES

Welcome to the zone where we're drawing lines, setting limits, and declaring, "This is my space, and I'm going to protect it like a queen guards her castle." Yep, we're talking about boundaries—the VIP ropes for your mental and emotional space.

So, what are boundaries? Think of them as the velvet ropes in the VIP section of your life. They're the rules you set to protect your energy, time, and peace. Boundaries are like the bodyguards of your well-being, and trust me, you're the VIP in this scenario.

Now, why are boundaries so crucial for self-care? Imagine this: You're throwing a party, and everyone's invited. But wait, if you let everyone in without a plan, chaos ensues, right? Boundaries are like the guest list for your mental and emotional party. They ensure only the good vibes get through, and the energy remains on point.

Just like a queen has rules for her castle, you've got rules for your mental and emotional kingdom. It's not about being rigid; it's about creating an environment where you can flourish. Setting boundaries is an act of self-love, saying, "I value myself enough to protect my peace."

Now, let's talk about the boundaries blueprint. It's like designing the floor plan of your emotional palace. Identify what's non-negotiable, where you need a little extra security, and where you can invite more positive energy.

Keep in mind that boundaries are not restrictions; they're the keys to your kingdom. Boundaries are the love letters you write to yourself, promising to honor and protect your mental and emotional well-being.

So, grab your crown, let's set those boundaries, and show the world that your castle is a fortress of self-love.

Prioritize Your Time and Energy

In a world where work can sometimes feel like an endless marathon, it's crucial to set boundaries to protect your time and energy. You can establish clear boundaries between work and personal life. Say "no" to the 24/7 hustle and allow yourself the space to recharge. This not only boosts productivity but also enhances your overall well-being.

Preserve Your Inner Peace

It's essential to strike a balance between being there for others and taking care of ourselves. By asserting the need for personal time, you deepen your friendships and preserve your inner peace. Remember, setting boundaries in your personal relationships is an act of self-love. It allows you to be present for others while also ensuring your well-being remains a priority.

Reclaim Your Mental Space

In today's world of constant digital connectivity, it's easy to become overwhelmed by the ceaseless buzz of social media. You can designate specific times for digital interaction and carve out moments for relaxation and real-world experiences. By doing so, you protect your mental health and rediscover the joys of offline living.

Remember, boundaries are not barriers; they're bridges to a more balanced, fulfilling life. They're the velvet rope that turns chaos into harmony, the life upgrade we all need. Set those boundaries like the queen you are, as you take control of your time, energy, and happiness.

Think about where you could use a little VIP treatment in your life. Is it work, relationships, or maybe reclaiming some "me-time"? Remember, setting boundaries is like having a personal bouncer for your soul.

Your well-being is like a VIP guest at your party, and we're not letting anyone crash it. It's time to set boundaries like a boss and declare, "My mental and emotional space is sacred." Your peace is a priority, not a luxury.

Think of setting boundaries as your grand coronation ceremony. It's your moment to step into your power and declare, "I am the queen of my life, and my boundaries are the crown jewels." You deserve to feel respected, heard, and valued.

Let's get personal, sis. Where in your life could you use a little boundary magic?

1. **Identify Your VIPs**: What areas of your life need some velvet ropes? Pinpoint the situations or relationships that could use a touch of boundary.
2. **Define Your Castle Rules**: What's non-negotiable for you? Whether it's taking a guilt-free break or expressing your needs in a relationship, set rules that align with your values.

Communication is Key: Let your VIPs know about the royal decree. Communicate your boundaries with love and clarity. Remember, it's not about shutting others out; it's about inviting in what truly serves you.

Your Throne Awaits: As you embark on this boundary-setting journey, envision yourself sitting on a throne of self-love and empowerment. You've got this, Queen! Your well-being is your kingdom, and boundaries are the jewels that make it shine.

Your well-being matters, and it's time to rule your world with the grace and power of a true boss!

Now that you're armed with the royal decree to set boundaries like a boss, let's dive into the art of expressing those needs with grace, sass, and a sprinkle of wisdom.

Rule #1: The Art of '*I Feel*' Statements: Expressing your needs is like crafting a masterpiece, and '*I feel*' statements are your paintbrush. Instead of saying, "You always..." or "You never...," try "*I feel*" statements. For example, "I feel overwhelmed when..." or "I feel happiest when..." It keeps the conversation focused on your feelings, avoiding blame-game drama.

Rule #2: The Power of '*I Need*' Requests: Queens, don't shy away from saying what you need. It's not about being demanding; it's about honoring yourself. So, go ahead and say, "I need some quiet time right now," or "I need your support in this." Boldly claiming your needs is a boss move.

Rule #3: Setting Clear Expectations: Ever had that moment when someone didn't get the memo? Avoid the confusion by setting clear expectations. Let them know what you need and what you expect. It's like sending a royal invitation to your castle—clear, concise, and oh-so-regal.

Rule #4: The Gentle Art of Saying 'No': Saying 'no' isn't rejection; it's self-love. Practice the gentle 'no' with phrases like, "I appreciate the offer, but my plate is full right now," or "I need to prioritize my well-being at the moment." It's a polite yet firm way of honoring your boundaries.

Rule #5: Embrace the Pause Button: In the heat of a moment, it's okay to hit the pause button. If a conversation is becoming overwhelming, take a breath and say, "Can we revisit this when I've had a moment to collect my thoughts?" It's a power move, ensuring your responses are thoughtful and intentional.

Remember, communication is the heartbeat of boundaries. Expressing your needs isn't a sign of weakness; it's a testament to your strength and self-awareness. So, go ahead, and communicate your needs like the boss you are!

Remember, Queen, that your kingdom is built on clear communication.

Now, let's talk about assertiveness, the secret to setting boundaries without losing your crown. It's all about owning your power with grace, and I'm here to let you know how to do it without breaking a sweat.

Rule #1: The Power of the 'Firm, Not Fierce' Approach: Being assertive doesn't mean being fierce like a lion (unless that's your vibe!). It's about being firm, like a queen who knows her worth. Picture this: Your friend invites you to yet another last-minute event, and you're swamped. Instead of saying yes and stressing, assertively say, "I appreciate the invite, but I already have plans. Let's plan for another time." Firm, not fierce.

Rule #2: The Elegant 'I' Statements: Assertiveness is like a dance, and 'I' statements are your elegant moves. If a colleague keeps dumping extra work on you, try, "I need to focus on my current tasks. Let's discuss how we can balance the workload." It's like a waltz of diplomacy, asserting your needs without stepping on toes.

Rule #3: The 'No Apologies' Zone: Queens, it's time to declare your space a 'No Apologies' zone. If you need time for yourself or have to decline an invitation, there's no need to apologize for honoring your boundaries. Saying, "I can't make it this time; I hope you understand," is assertive and unapologetic.

Rule #4: The Queenly Pause: Picture this scenario: Someone crosses a boundary, and instead of reacting, you give them the queenly pause. Take a breath and calmly say, "That comment wasn't acceptable. Let's keep our conversation respectful." It's assertiveness wrapped in regal composure.

Rule #5: The Art of 'I Deserve' Declarations: Remind yourself that you deserve to set boundaries. If someone questions your decision, confidently say, "I deserve to prioritize my well-being," or "I deserve to have my needs respected." Assertiveness is your right, not a request.

Being assertive isn't about being aggressive—it's about standing tall in your power.

Guess what? Your voice is a symphony, and it deserves to be heard loud and clear! Let's look at ways of confidently communicating your desires because, honey, you're the conductor of this orchestra.

The Power of Clarity: Imagine your desires are stars in the night sky—bright, beautiful, and unapologetic. When expressing your desires, be crystal clear. No need for constellations when you've got straightforward communication. Say, "I would love to spend more quality time together," or "I need support with this project." Your wishes are commands!

Confidence, Not Cockiness: Confidence is your BFF, but we're leaving cockiness at the door. Picture this: You're expressing your desires at work, wanting to lead a project. Instead of saying, "I'm the best for the job," try, "I believe my skills align well with leading this project." Confidence shines without overshadowing others.

The 'I Believe in Me' Mantra: Repeat after me: "I believe in me!" Your desires matter, and so does your self-belief. Whether it's in your personal or professional life, say, "I believe in my ability to achieve this," or "I believe I deserve this opportunity." Your voice is the melody of belief.

The 'No Holding Back' Approach: Your desires are not a secret society; they're meant to be shared boldly. When discussing your desires, say it like you mean it. "I've been dreaming of taking on more responsibilities," or "I've set my eyes on that promotion." Don't hold back, this is your time to shine!

The Queenly Gratitude: Expressing desires doesn't mean forgetting gratitude. When someone supports your desires, say, "Thank you for understanding my goals," or "I appreciate your support in making this happen." Gratitude is the glitter that makes your desires sparkle.

Your voice deserves the spotlight. So, stand tall, speak confidently, and let the world hear your desires. You're the lead singer of your life's anthem, and the world is your stage!

Chapter 7
CULTIVATING SISTERHOOD

Let's talk about something so essential, cultivating the most fabulous support system ever: sisterhood! Imagine it as a blend of wisdom, laughter, and a touch of magic. Some primary rules of sisterhood include:

Sisterhood Rule #1: The Power of Understanding: Ever had a friend who just gets you? Sisterhood is all about that deep, soulful understanding. It's like your friend knowing you need a vent session before you even say a word. Sisters uplift by truly getting each other.

Sisterhood Rule #2: Laughter Therapy: Laughter is the best medicine, and with your sisters, it's a whole comedy show! Picture this: You're stressed about work, and your sister sends a meme that has you in stitches. Laughter is the glue that keeps sisterhood strong—keep those laughs coming!

Sisterhood Rule #3: The 'Lift Each Other Up' Vow: In the kingdom of sisterhood, there's no room for competition; only celebration! When your sister succeeds, you celebrate her. When she stumbles, you offer a hand. Together, you rise. It's a 'lift each other up' vow we all need in our lives.

Sisterhood Rule #4: No Judgment Zone: Sisterhood is a judge-free zone. Picture this: You've made a decision that might seem a bit wild to others. Instead of judgment, your sister says, "You go, girl!" Sisters empower without question; they're the ultimate hype squad.

Sisterhood Rule #5: The Magical Sisterhood Circle: Imagine sitting in a circle with your sisters, each bringing their unique magic. This is your sisterhood circle, where dreams are shared, advice is given, and love is sprinkled generously. Together, you create a force that's unstoppable.

Sisterhood is a treasure chest of love, understanding, and endless empowerment. So, let's hold each other close, uplift one another, and remember, together, we're a powerful team to be reckoned with!

Let me tell you something beautiful—you and your sisters are like a bouquet of flowers. Each petal unique, but together, you create a masterpiece.

Imagine a world where every woman embraces the beauty of sisterhood. It's like having a squad that has your back through thick and thin. We celebrate wins together, lift each other up when we stumble, and sprinkle encouragement on each other's dreams. Sisterhood is the ultimate celebration of womanhood!

Picture this: You, your sisters, and a mountain of dreams to conquer. Together, we rise like a pool of strong, fearless, and fabulous women. Your victories are our victories, and your joy is our joy. It's a celebration where the champagne flows, and the laughter echoes.

Sisterhood is not just a bond; it's a movement. It's the power of collective strength, wisdom, and love. When one sister shines, we all bask in her glow. So, let's celebrate the invisible power that is sisterhood!

Picture this: a world where every woman is a cheerleader for her sisters, a hype woman for their dreams. It's time to talk about the magic that happens when we lift each other up!

Ever had a friend who made you feel like you could conquer the world? That's the magic of uplifting! It's not just a compliment here or there; it's a genuine belief in the power and potential of your sisters. When one rises, we all rise. It's the ultimate 'lift as you climb' philosophy.

Imagine handing a cape to your sister and telling her she's a superhero. That's empowerment, my queen! It's about recognizing the strength, talents, and beauty in each other and being the wind beneath each other's wings. When your sister feels invincible, that's when the magic happens.

Uplifting and empowering aren't solo acts; they're a sisterhood affair. It's the joy of seeing your sister slay her goals and being the loudest cheerleader in her success parade. When we unite in lifting each other, the collective energy is unstoppable!

Every woman is a unique masterpiece, and it's time to celebrate that uniqueness. Your sister might be fierce in the boardroom, while another is a creative genius. Embrace the differences, celebrate the quirks, and empower each other to shine in your own brilliant way.

Uplifting and empowering are like secret ingredients in the sisterhood potion. So, let's keep spreading that magic dust, cheering for each other, and empowering our fellow queens. Together, we create a symphony of strength, resilience, and unbridled fabulousness!

Now that we're soaking in the power of sisterhood, let's chat about how we can sprinkle that magic everywhere—whether it's at work, in our social circles, or just cheering on a sister from afar.

Office Majesty: Ever been in a meeting where your sister pitched a fantastic idea? Be the first to show your support! Acknowledge her brilliance in that Zoom chat like it's the hottest gossip in town. Lift her up in the workplace and watch the whole office vibe change.

Social Squad Goals: Planning a girls' night out? Or maybe a virtual catch-up? Be the one who hypes up your sisters like they're walking the red carpet. Share the spotlight, shower them with compliments, and create an atmosphere where everyone shines. It's a squad, not a competition!

Virtual Cheers and High-Fives: Distance can't dim the glow of sisterhood. Send voice notes, text messages, or even memes that scream, "You're killing it, Queen!" A well-timed emoji can turn a regular day into a celebration of sisterly love.

Goals, Dreams, and Victory Dances: Your sister just hit a personal milestone? Cue the victory dance! Whether it's a promotion, a fitness goal, or conquering a fear, be the one doing the happy dance in her honor. Celebrate her victories as if they were your own.

Random Acts of Kindness: Ever received a surprise cup of coffee or an encouraging note? Spread that joy! Surprise your sisters with little gestures that say, "I see you, and you're amazing." The smallest acts can create the biggest smiles.

Supporting and encouraging our sisters is like creating an area of love and empowerment. So, let's keep the compliments flowing, the cheers booming, and the virtual high-fives going. In the world of sisterhood, every gesture counts!

Sister, the world needs more of your magic, your support, and your uplifting spirit. So, here's the call to action: Be the queen who supports, encourages, and uplifts her fellow queens. The journey of empowerment is a collective one, and you're a crucial part of this grand sisterhood ensemble.

Make supporting and encouraging second nature. It's not a one-time thing; it's a lifestyle. Compliment freely, celebrate sincerely, and share those good vibes. Your love and encouragement can create a ripple effect that transforms lives.

In a world that sometimes tries to pit women against each other, be the one who builds bridges of support. Break down those walls of competition and replace them with doorways to collaboration and sisterly love. We're better together!

Queens don't compete; they elevate. Your success doesn't diminish mine, and vice versa. Let's commit to lifting each other higher, celebrating every victory, and turning every setback into a setup for a major comeback.

Remember this: Queens support Queens. It's not just a catchy phrase; it's a powerful truth. So, let's keep this sisterhood magic alive and thriving. Your support matters more than you know, and together, we'll conquer anything life throws our way!

Chapter 8
GOAL SETTING AND ACHIEVEMENT

Let's talk goals—those magical little roadmaps that take us from where we are to where we want to be. Now, I know setting goals can feel a bit like planning a cross-country road trip with a GPS that only speaks in riddles. But fear not, my fabulous friend, because we're about to break it all down into bite-sized, achievable chunks.

Setting SMART Goals: A Roadmap for Queens

S - Specific: Your goals need to be as clear as that picture-perfect sunset. Instead of saying, "I want to be successful," get specific. Define what success means to you. Are we talking a corner office, a thriving business, or mastering that TikTok dance? Clarity is key, Queen!

M - Measurable: Let's make those goals measurable, like trying to figure out how many scoops of ice cream you can balance on a cone without it toppling over. If your goal is to enhance your career, ask yourself: How will I measure success? Is it a certain income, a number of clients, or a specific position?

A - Achievable: Think of your goals as fabulous shoes—chic but comfortable. They should stretch you a bit, but if they pinch too much, we might need a new pair. Make sure your goals are challenging yet attainable. Being a CEO by next week might be a tad ambitious, but climbing the ladder step by step is totally doable.

R - Relevant: Let's keep it real, sis. Your goals need to align with your values and passions. If your heart isn't in it, even a gold-plated achievement won't bring the satisfaction you crave. Ensure your goals are relevant to your journey and light that fire within you.

T - Time-Bound: Queens don't wait around; they set deadlines! Give your goals a timeline. Whether it's six months or two years, having that finish line in sight adds a dash of urgency and keeps you focused. Time is a valuable asset, and we're not wasting a second of it.

So, there you have it—a crash course in setting SMART goals. It's like designing your custom-made gown for the grand ball of life. Now, grab your scepter (or maybe just a pen) and start mapping out your royal route to success.

Let's talk about dreams—the kind that dance in your head with a burst of color. Now, I know your dreams are big, bold, and as dazzling as a disco ball. But here's the thing, darling: those dreamy dance moves need a starting groove. So, grab your invisible disco shoes, and let's set some goals that sync perfectly with your fabulous vision.

Dream Big, Start Small: Your Goals, Your Symphony

Picture this: your dreams are a glittering disco ball, reflecting the myriad possibilities of your fabulous future. Now, don't get me wrong, dreaming big is our jam, our ultimate playlist. Your dreams are the headlining act, and we're about to make them the concert of a lifetime.

Think of goal setting as the choreography to your dreams' electrifying music. It's about finding the right rhythm, the perfect steps that lead you from where you are to where you want to be. So, put on your dancing shoes (real or imaginary) and let's create a goal-setting routine that's uniquely yours.

Your goals should be the dance moves that complement your dreams' melody. Start by envisioning the final pose of each dance —those big dreams materializing into reality. Whether it's conquering the business world or mastering a new skill, let your goals be the steps that get you there.

Start Small, Slay Big: Now, here's the tea, love. Starting small doesn't mean dreaming small; it means breaking down those dazzling dreams into manageable, achievable steps. Imagine it like learning a dance routine—one step at a time until you're twirling in the spotlight.

Aligning Goals with Your Vision: Your goals should be the dance partners that perfectly match the rhythm of your dreams. If your dream is to own a business empire, your goals might include learning the ropes, networking, and conquering one sector at a time. It's about crafting a sequence that leads to your grand finale.

It's time to set goals that groove with the rhythm of your dreams. Dream big, start small, and soon you'll be dancing to the beat of your own success. Your dreams are within reach, and together, we're about to create a masterpiece.

We've dreamed big, started small, and now it's time to map out the journey. Imagine it like planning the most fabulous road trip of your life—with plenty of snacks, of course.

Dream Big, Snack Big, Slay Big: Your Goals, Your Journey

Dreams Like a Snack Buffet: Okay, picture your dreams as a mouthwatering buffet spread. Every dream is a delicious dish waiting for you to savor. Now, we're about to create the ultimate feast—one step at a time. But before we dive into the details, let me tell you, your dreams are worth every bite.

Map Out Your Fabulous Journey: Just like any epic road trip, achieving your dreams requires a roadmap. We're not talking about a boring, foldable map you struggle to read. Nah, honey, we're creating a vibrant, glittery GPS to guide you through every twist and turn of your journey.

Step-by-Step Fabulosity: You know how in every great adventure movie, the hero takes one step at a time to conquer the impossible? Well, you're the star of your own blockbuster, and it's time to break down those dreams into steps. Each step is a scene, and together, they create the blockbuster of your life.

Creating Your Goal Roadmap: Imagine your goals as the pit stops along this fabulous road trip. From learning new skills to conquering challenges, each goal is a milestone on your journey to greatness. I want you to outline these goals like you're planning the most glamorous itinerary.

The Power of Milestones: Milestones are like the dazzling landmarks on your journey. They mark your progress, and each one brings you closer to the grand finale. Celebrate them like pit stops at a fabulous spa or a roadside café serving the most divine treats. You're making history, Diva!

Adjust the Volume, Not the Goal: Now, I know sometimes life throws curveballs, and the road gets a bit bumpy. But don't you worry, Queen. You're the DJ of this journey, and you can adjust the volume, not the goal. Stay flexible, stay fierce, and keep grooving to your own rhythm.

Your Road Trip Playlist: What's a road trip without a killer playlist? Your goals are the tracks that make this journey unforgettable. From the motivational anthem to the empowerment ballad, choose the tunes that resonate with your soul. Because, baby, you're the rock star on this ride.

Your dreams are the destination, and we've got the roadmap. Dream big, snack big, slay big—you've got this, and I'm right here cheering you on from the passenger seat.

Now that we've got our goals all dolled up, it's time to give them the VIP treatment. We're talking about the full glam—milestones, potential challenges, and strategies to conquer them. Trust me, this is where the real magic happens.

Milestones: Your Glamorous Checkpoints

Imagine your journey as a red carpet event, and each milestone is a fabulous checkpoint where you strike a pose and soak in the applause. These are your victories, Diva, and they deserve to be celebrated like winning an Oscar.

1. **Goal Glamour Shots:** Let's give each goal a glamour shot. Picture it like a dazzling photoshoot where your goals are the supermodels. Strike a pose for each one, and let them shine. These shots will be the envy of every other goal out there!

2. **Milestones on the Red Carpet:** Your milestones are the celebrities of this red carpet. From learning a new skill to conquering a fear, each achievement is a star-studded moment. Take a moment to appreciate your journey, Queen— you're the A-lister here.

3. **Celebrity Endorsements (From You!):** Endorse your milestones like a true celebrity. Give them the spotlight they deserve. Share your victories with pride, and let the world know that you're a force to be reckoned with. Your journey is making headlines!

Potential Challenges: The Plot Twists

Just like in a blockbuster movie, every journey has its plot twists. But don't you worry, we're the directors of this show, and we've got the script ready. Let's anticipate those challenges and show them who's boss.

1. **Spotting the Potential Villains:** Identify those challenges like the villains they are. Whether it's time constraints, self-doubt, or unexpected hurdles, name them. This is your blockbuster, and you're not letting any villain steal the spotlight.

2. **Scripting Your Comeback:** Every hero needs a killer comeback, and that's you, Queen. Script your response to each challenge. Turn those setbacks into comebacks that leave everyone in awe. You're the writer, and this is your masterpiece.

3. **Supporting Cast (Your Strategies):** Your supporting cast is your strategies for overcoming challenges. Whether it's seeking advice, finding a mentor, or practicing self-care, these strategies are the allies that help you triumph over adversity.

Strategies: The Behind-the-Scenes Magic

Now, let's dive into the behind-the-scenes magic that makes your journey extraordinary. These strategies are the special effects, the stunt doubles, and the magic that turns dreams into reality.

1. **Stunt Doubles (Backup Plans):** Just like in a high-stakes scene, you need stunt doubles—backup plans for when things get intense. Plan B, C, and D are your stunt doubles. They ensure the show goes on, no matter what.
2. **Special Effects (Your Unique Spark):** Your unique spark is the special effect that sets your journey apart. Whether it's a skill you bring to the table or a support system you've built, these special effects add the wow factor to your goals.
3. **Magic Moments (Rewards and Celebrations):** Celebrate your victories like magic moments. Treat yourself to a spa day, a favorite meal, or a dance party in your living room. These moments of celebration are the enchanting spells that keep you motivated.

Your goals are now the stars of a blockbuster, and you're the director calling the shots. Milestones, challenges, and strategies—this is where the real drama unfolds, and you, my dear, are the leading lady.

- Picture this—a runway just for you, Queen. Each step is a strut of victory. Hold your head high, own your achievements, and let the world witness your fabulousness. Strut, and don't forget to toss that hair back.

- Create a confidence playlist for these victorious moments. From Beyoncé to Aretha, let the divas serenade you as you conquer your goals. You're the star of this show, and your playlist should reflect it.

- Take spontaneous dance breaks to celebrate those wins. Break out into your favorite dance move—whether it's a twirl, a shimmy, or the moonwalk. Your journey, your dance floor.

Victory Chants:

1. Repeat after me, "Every step I take is a victory." Whether it's a small shuffle or a giant leap, every step counts. Your journey is a dance, and each step brings you closer to the grand finale.
2. Let's walk this path together, Diva. Hand in hand, step by step, we're making strides. Your victories inspire others, just as theirs inspire you. This is a collective journey, and we're in it together.
3. The path may have twists, turns, and unexpected choreography, but always move forward. Victory is in the progress, not just the destination. Keep strutting, dancing, and sashaying, Queen.

Every goal you set, every milestone you achieve—it's your story unfolding on the big screen. So, grab your popcorn, because the best scenes are yet to come.

Chapter 9
MINDFULNESS AND SELF-CARE

Picture this: a spa day for your soul, a royal decree for tranquility, and a crown of self-love sparkling on your head. We're about to dive deep into the kingdom of self-care. So, loosen that crown, kick off those heels (or sneakers), and let's embark on a journey of pampering fit for a queen.

The Royal Decree of Self-Care:

- **Mind, Body, and Soul:** Self-care isn't just about face masks and bubble baths; it's a holistic journey. It's feeding your mind with positivity, fueling your body with nourishment, and soothing your soul with moments of pure bliss. It's a three-course meal for the queen within.

- **Boundaries, Darling:** Establishing boundaries isn't just about saying no; it's about saying yes to yourself. It's like having your own royal guards, protecting your peace and ensuring your energy is reserved for what truly matters. Bow down to the art of saying, "This is for me."

- **Laughter, the Best Medicine:** Your laugh is the melody of your soul, and laughter? That's your daily dose of medicine. So, surround yourself with joy, throw in a pinch of humor, and let the echoes of laughter reverberate through your kingdom. After all, a merry heart does good like a medicine.

Soulful Pampering:

- Light a candle, sip your favorite tea, and have a heart-to-heart with yourself. Reflect on your triumphs, acknowledge your challenges, and remind yourself of the queen you are. It's a date with the most important person in your life—YOU.

- Immerse yourself in sensory delights. Whether it's the aroma of your favorite candle, the touch of soft fabrics, or the taste of a decadent treat, let your senses revel in the richness of the experience. Pamper yourself like the royalty you are.

- In the chaos of life, steal moments of mindfulness. Whether it's a few deep breaths, a mindful walk, or just being present in the now, these moments are your crowning glory. Own them with regal poise.

As we unfold the royal tapestry of self-care, remember, this isn't indulgence; it's a necessity. You're not just maintaining, darling; you're flourishing.

Amidst the hustle and bustle of daily life, dedicating a few minutes to meditation can serve as your anchor. Inhale courage, exhale stress, and let mindfulness become your daily ritual. It's a powerful tool for reigning over your realm with grace and calmness.

Laughter isn't just medicine; it's a secret potion for a happier existence. Whether it's through a funny podcast, sharing jokes, or indulging in goofy dance moves, prioritize moments of joy in your daily routine. A dose of laughter is your key to a more joyful reign.

Nurturing yourself is a royal duty, just as important as any other responsibility. Steal moments for self-care – a bubble bath, a solo coffee date, or any activity that brings you joy and rejuvenation. By prioritizing self-care, you reign supreme in your life.

Self-care isn't selfish; it's survival. It's the secret sauce to a life well-lived. Your well-being is not negotiable.

In a world that demands so much, remember, you're allowed to demand a little TLC for yourself. Self-care isn't a luxury; it's a necessity. Your well-being is not just a priority; it's a crown jewel. Your well-being is a crown that, when worn with mindfulness, laughter, and self-care, can truly make us feel like royalty in our own lives.

I've curated a spread of self-care routines for you.

1. Morning Majesty: Rise and Shine Routine: Start your day like the royalty you are. Whether it's a five-minute gratitude journal, a dance session to your favorite tunes, or simply sipping your coffee with intention – let the morning set the tone for your queendom.

2. Midday Recharge: Office Oasis Edition: Even in the midst of a bustling workday, you can steal moments of tranquility. Try quick mindfulness exercises, a power nap, or a brisk walk. Your throne at the office deserves a sprinkle of self-care magic.

3. Evening Elevation: Unwind Like Royalty: As the day winds down, let your self-care rituals blossom. Indulge in a warm bath, a good book, or a soothing skincare routine. Your evening routine is the royal icing on your self-care cake.

4. Weekend Royal Retreat: Big or Small, It's All About You:
Weekends are the sanctuary of self-care. Whether it's a grand spa day, a nature hike, or binge-watching your favorite shows in cozy PJs, claim this time as yours. Weekends are where the magic happens, Queen.

5. Everyday Elegance: Micro-Moments of Magic: Sprinkle micro-moments of self-care throughout your day. It could be a deep breath, a mindful pause, or a quick affirmation. Remember, it's not always about grand gestures but the everyday elegance of taking care of yourself.

Remember, this self-care buffet is all about what nourishes your soul. Mix and match, find your favorites, and create a routine that feels as decadent as a crown on your head. Self-care isn't one-size-fits-all; it's tailor-made for you.

Let's create your personalized self-care plan – the sacred scroll that outlines how you'll shower yourself with love, kindness, and all the good vibes.

1. Know Thyself: Reflect on what makes your heart dance, your soul sing, and your spirit soar. Are you a morning person or a night owl? Do you find solace in nature or in the bustling city? Knowing thyself is the first step to curating your royal self-care journey.

2. Mix and Match: Your self-care plan is a masterpiece, darling, and like any masterpiece, it's made up of various strokes. Mix and match different activities – physical, mental, and emotional. Blend moments of solitude with social escapades. The key is finding the perfect blend that suits your queendom.

3. **Prioritize Yourself: Your time is precious. When crafting your self-care plan, prioritize activities that truly resonate with you. Whether it's a weekly spa night, a monthly adventure, or daily affirmations, let it be all about you – your desires, your well-being, your majesty.

4. **Flexibility Is Key: Life is like a jazz melody, full of unexpected twists and turns. Your self-care plan should dance to the rhythm of your life. Be flexible, adapt, and flow. If a grand spa day turns into a cozy movie night, let it be – it's all part of the royal experience.

5. **Celebrate Your Wins: As you embark on this self-care journey, celebrate the wins, big or small. Did you complete a week of daily affirmations? Treat yourself. Did you conquer a fear? Cheers to your bravery. Your self-care plan is a journey of victories; make sure to revel in them.

Crafting a personalized self-care plan is like designing your own castle – a sanctuary for your well-being. So, grab your quill, let your imagination run wild, and pledge allegiance to your own care.

Life can be a tumultuous symphony, with responsibilities, expectations, and the occasional plot twist that keeps us on our toes. Yet, in the midst of the chaos, find those moments for yourself – your solo in the grand performance. You deserve a spotlight that's entirely yours.

Amidst the demands of family, work, and the general whirlwind of life, remember, you are worthy of your own time. Whether it's a stolen moment of serenity during sunrise or a cozy evening wrapped in self-love, make time for the one who matters most – You.

Your cup must overflow so you can generously pour into others. So, in the chaos, find your sanctuary, and let self-care be your guiding mantra.

Here's to finding your moments, embracing your solo, and recognizing that in the symphony of life, you are the music, the rhythm, and the melody. Cheers to you!

Remember – in the chaos of life, find those moments for yourself. They are the jewels in your crown, the treasures that make your reign truly majestic.

Chapter 10
HEALTH AND WELL-BEING

You see, our bodies and minds are like two peas in a pod, and they have this incredible connection that we should all know about.

Understanding the Mind-Body Connection

Now, let's get down to business and talk about the intricate relationship between mental and physical health. Picture this: your mind is the captain of the ship, and your body is the ship itself. They sail through life together, and when one isn't doing so hot, the other feels the waves too.

Think about a time when you were super stressed. I know, it's not the most glamorous memory, but stay with me. Your mind was probably racing, right? Well, that stress isn't just a mental thing; it can have very real physical consequences. Your heart might start racing, your stomach feels like a rollercoaster, and you might even get a pesky headache. Yep, that's the mind-body connection in action.

Emotional Well-being and Physical Health

But guess what, my fabulous friend? It goes both ways! Just like stress can mess with your physical health, your emotional well-being can do wonders for your body too. When you're feeling on top of the world, your body is like, "We got this, Queen!" You might have more energy, sleep better, and even notice your skin glowing with happiness.

So, it's a two-way street. When you treat your body right, it can do wonders for your mental health, and when you're in a good headspace, your body thanks you in more ways than you can imagine.

Let's have a heart-to-heart about something that's no stranger to any of us: stress. Life can be a rollercoaster, and sometimes it feels like we're on the loop-de-loops more than we'd like. But you know what? We've got some serious power to tackle that stress head-on.

Stress is like that uninvited guest at the party that just won't leave, right? It sneaks in, crashes the scene, and suddenly your whole vibe is off. But here's the thing: stress doesn't just mess with your mind; it plays tricks on your body too.

When stress barges in, your body goes into full-on alert mode. Your heart races, muscles tense up, and that little knot in your stomach? Yeah, that's stress doing its thing. It's like your body's way of saying, "Hey, we need to deal with this!"

Mind-Body Harmony with Stress Management
Now, I've got some awesome news for you, Queen. We're not just here to moan about stress; we're here to conquer it! And guess what? You don't need any superhero capes for this one. Nope, all you need are some nifty stress management techniques.

Let's talk mindfulness, meditation, and deep breathing exercises – the ultimate stress-busting trio. They're like your trusty sidekicks in the battle against stress. When you practice mindfulness, you're basically telling your mind, "Hey, we're here, right now, in this moment." It's a beautiful way to calm the storm inside.

Meditation? Oh, honey, it's like a mini vacation for your brain. It helps you hit that mental reset button, leaving you feeling refreshed and ready to take on the world. And those deep breaths? They're pure magic. Deep breathing exercises can instantly calm your body down, like a soothing lullaby for your soul.

So, Queen, when life throws those stress grenades your way, remember, you've got the tools to defuse them. It's all about finding what works best for you and making it a part of your daily routine. Your mind and body will thank you, and you'll be back to your fabulous self in no time.

Let's chat about something that'll give you those good vibes from head to toe – exercise. I know, I know, it can feel like just one more thing to add to your already packed schedule, but trust me, this is a game-changer.

Sweat It Out, Girl!
Now, picture this: you're crushing your favorite workout, beads of sweat glistening like diamonds, and that Beyoncé playlist blaring through your earbuds. That's the magic of exercise! It's not just about getting that summer body; it's about feeding your mind and soul too.

When you exercise, your body releases these magical chemicals called endorphins. They're like your body's own happy pills. Endorphins flood your system, and suddenly, the world seems a little brighter, challenges feel more conquerable, and stress? Well, it takes a backseat.

A Busy Queen's Guide to Fitness

I get it, sis, life's hectic, and it can be tough to squeeze in a workout. But here's the tea – you don't need to run a marathon or spend hours in the gym. Nope, not at all. Exercise can be as simple as a brisk walk, a quick dance session in your living room, or even a fun fitness class with friends.

The key is finding something you enjoy. If you love it, you'll make time for it. And don't forget, workouts can double as "me time." It's a chance to clear your mind, focus on yourself, and escape the daily chaos.

But here's the golden nugget, Queens: consistency is key. Even if it's just 15 minutes a day, regular exercise can work wonders for your mental health. It boosts your confidence, reduces stress, and helps you sleep like a baby. Plus, that post-workout glow? It's real, and it's fabulous.

So, let's make a pact. Promise yourself to move that gorgeous body of yours regularly. Whether it's a morning yoga flow, an evening dance party, or a lunch break stroll, let's get that blood pumping and those endorphins soaring. Your mind and body will thank you for it.

Alright, my beautiful Queens, let's dive into something that's near and dear to our hearts – food! I mean, who doesn't love a good meal, right? But here's the tea: what you eat has a major impact on your mental and physical well-being.

Food is Fuel, Honey

Think of your body as a high-performance machine, and food is the fuel that powers it. If you're pumping junk into your engine, well, you can't expect it to run smoothly, can you? But when you give it the good stuff, the results are phenomenal.

Now, I'm not here to tell you to ditch the treats and live on kale alone (although kale can be pretty fabulous). It's all about balance, Queen. Enjoy your pizza nights and indulge in that chocolate cake, but also make room for the good-for-you stuff.

Making Wise Choices

You know those leafy greens, vibrant fruits, lean proteins, and whole grains? They're your allies, your confidantes, your beauty secret. They nourish your body from the inside out, giving you energy, boosting your mood, and keeping those brain cells firing.

But let's keep it real. Life throws us curveballs, and sometimes, we find ourselves drowning our stress in a pint of ice cream or stress-eating a bag of chips. It happens to the best of us! The key is not beating yourself up about it. Instead, let's make an effort to balance those indulgences with nourishing meals.

Defeating Dietary Demons

Now, I know we all have our dietary demons – those cravings that seem impossible to resist. Whether it's late-night snacking or emotional eating, we've been there. But here's the secret weapon: awareness.

When you catch yourself reaching for that bag of chips, pause for a second. Ask yourself, "Am I really hungry, or am I just stressed?" Sometimes, it's not your stomach that's empty; it's your heart. In those moments, find healthier ways to cope with your emotions – a chat with a friend, a journaling session, or a quick dance break.

You deserve the royal treatment, and that includes nourishing your body with love. So, let's make a pact to make wiser food choices, one meal at a time. Remember, it's not about perfection; it's about progress. You've got this!

You know that feeling when you wake up after a night of blissful sleep? It's like you're ready to conquer the world, right? Well, that's what we're diving into now – the importance of quality sleep and how it's the secret sauce to keeping both your mind and body in tip-top shape.

The Royal Recharge

Imagine your body as a smartphone, and sleep is the charger. Just like your phone needs juice to function, your body needs quality sleep to repair and recharge. It's during those nighttime hours that your mind tidies up, your cells regenerate, and your energy gets restored.

But, oh honey, I know the struggle is real. In today's hustle-and-bustle world, it's easy to skip out on sleep or have those restless nights filled with tossing, turning, and checking your social media at 2 a.m. Am I right?

Let's break it down, Queen. Quality sleep isn't about the quantity of hours you clock in; it's about the quality of those hours. So, how do we ensure you're getting the royal treatment?

1. **Sleep Hygiene**: Think of this as your bedtime routine for grown-ups. It includes creating a relaxing pre-sleep ritual. Dim those lights, put away the gadgets, and opt for calming activities like reading, gentle stretches, or a warm bath. It's all about signaling to your body, "Hey, it's time to wind down."

2. **A Sleep-Supportive Environment**: Your sleep space should be your sanctuary. Make sure your mattress is comfy, the room is dark, and the temperature is just right – not too hot and not too cold. And, oh, invest in some cozy bedding. You deserve to feel like a queen when you hit the hay!

3. **Consistent Sleep Schedule**: Your body loves routine, so try to stick to a regular sleep schedule, even on weekends. It helps regulate your internal clock and makes falling asleep and waking up easier.

4. **Banish the Blue Light**: You know that blue light from your phone and laptop? It messes with your sleep hormone, melatonin. So, dim the screens a few hours before bedtime, and your sleep will thank you.

The Power of Naps

Now, don't get me wrong; I'm a firm believer in the power of a good cat nap! But when it comes to nighttime sleep, quality reigns supreme. If you're struggling with sleep, consult with a healthcare professional. Sometimes, there are underlying issues that need addressing.

Remember, my Queen, you deserve those restful, rejuvenating nights of sleep. It's like hitting the reset button on your fabulous self!

We've covered a lot on taking care of our physical health, but you know what's just as important? Our mental health, honey! It's time we shine a light on it because, after all, being fabulous means taking care of our minds as well as our bodies.

Your Mental Crown Matters Too

Think of your mind as your most precious crown, and girl, you need to keep it polished and shining! Our mental health is just as crucial as our physical well-being, and there's absolutely no shame in talking about it.

So, let's address something really important: the stigma around mental health issues. You see, society has thrown some shade on this topic for way too long. It's time we kick that stigma to the curb and bring mental health out of the shadows!

Recognizing the Red Flags

It's okay not to be okay sometimes. We all have our down days. But when those down days start to feel like a never-ending night, it's time to pay attention. Mental health concerns can manifest in various ways – mood swings, sleep disturbances, anxiety, or just an overwhelming feeling of not being yourself.

Now, I'm not a therapist, but I am your friend here to tell you this: there's no shame in asking for help. Just like you'd see a doctor for a physical issue, it's perfectly fine to seek help when your mental health needs a little TLC.

Don't go through tough times alone, sis! Reach out to your friends, your family, or a mental health professional.

CONCLUSION

As we journey through the final pages of Fearless Femininity, I want to take a moment to wrap our shared exploration of self-discovery, resilience, and sisterhood. What a ride it's been—a rollercoaster of emotions, a surge of empowerment, and a dance with the nuances of being beautifully, unapologetically you.

From the first chapter, where we embraced our imperfections, to the empowering narratives of women who turned challenges into triumphs, we've embarked on a transformative expedition. Each chapter, a steppingstone toward a more authentic, fearless version of ourselves. As we conclude, let's revisit the essence of our journey, celebrating the milestones and embracing the lessons learned.

Imperfections as Power

We began by acknowledging imperfections not as shortcomings but as unique brushstrokes on the canvas of our lives. Remember, Diva, it's these imperfections that add color to our stories, making each of us a masterpiece in the grand gallery of life.

Think of your quirks, your laughs, your scars as badges of honor, testaments to a life well-lived. The women we discussed, from celebrities to everyday heroines, all found strength and power in embracing their imperfections. They not only accepted but flaunted what society deemed flaws, turning them into defining features.

So, the next time you look in the mirror, see beyond what you think are flaws. Your reflection is a symphony of unique notes, creating a melody that only you can sing. Your imperfections are not blemishes; they are the punctuation marks that make your story uniquely yours.

Overcoming Self-Doubt

We unraveled the common thread that binds us all: the struggle to believe in ourselves.

We discovered the beauty of self-love, the strength in vulnerability, and the courage it takes to overcome the whispers of doubt. Whether you're a published author, a flight attendant, or a creative entrepreneur, your journey is a testament to your ability to conquer self-doubt.

So, dear Diva, the next time you find yourself standing at the intersection of fear and doubt, remember you have the power within to silence those doubts and march forward with the confidence of a queen.

Connecting Through Shared Experiences

We delved into relatable scenarios that many women can connect with—those moments of heartache, the hurdles of chasing dreams, the juggle of responsibilities, and the ever-elusive quest for balance. In those shared experiences, we found comfort, solidarity, and a reminder that we're never alone on this journey.

Think about the times you felt isolated, thinking no one could possibly understand. Our shared stories echo through the chapters, weaving a tapestry of shared experiences. Whether it's the challenge of setting boundaries, embracing authenticity, or celebrating the victories, we've walked this path together.

So, the next time life throws you a curveball, remember the community we've built here. Reach out to your sisters, share your stories, and find strength in the collective power of womanhood.

Unleashing the Power Within
Chapter after chapter, we unlocked the untapped potential within every woman. From discovering passions to identifying strengths, we've equipped ourselves with the tools to navigate this journey called life.

Diva, your strength is limitless. It's time to unleash it. The exercises, journal prompts, and reflections were not just words on pages—they were invitations to explore the depths of your potential. It's time to embark on the path of self-discovery, armed with the knowledge that your power is a force to be reckoned with.

Remember, you're not just a passenger in the journey of life; you're the captain, steering your ship through the storms and basking in the sunshine of your triumphs.

Celebrating Sisterhood
Our celebration of sisterhood was not just a feel-good sentiment; it was a call to action. We explored the unique support system women provide for each other, celebrated the beauty of sisterhood, and discussed the importance of uplifting and empowering fellow women.

Queens support Queens—it's not just a catchy phrase; it's a way of life. In a world that often pits women against each other, we stood together, recognizing that our collective success and empowerment amplify the strength of each individual.

So, the next time you see a sister struggling, lend a hand. When you witness a triumph, celebrate it as if it were your own. Our sisterhood is a force to be reckoned with, capable of breaking barriers, shattering ceilings, and creating a world where every woman can thrive.

Setting Goals and Dreaming Big

In our exploration of setting SMART goals and dreaming big, we painted a vivid picture of success. But remember, Diva, success is not a one-size-fits-all concept. It's a personal journey, a tailored suit crafted to fit your unique aspirations.

We outlined roadmaps, milestones, and strategies for overcoming challenges, encouraging you to walk your path at your pace. Your dreams are within reach, and we're here to cheer you on as you conquer every step forward.

Every victory, no matter how small, is a triumph. So, celebrate them. Revel in the joy of progress, for it's these steps that lead to the grand finale of your success story.

The Essence of Self-Care

As we dipped our toes into the waters of self-care, we discovered the rejuvenating power of mindfulness and the necessity of putting ourselves first. Your well-being, both mental and emotional, is not selfish; it's a priority. Through stories and practical routines, we explored ways to nurture the most important relationship—the one with yourself.

So, the next time life gets chaotic, find moments for yourself. Your deserve it, Diva. In the dance of life, make sure you save a few steps for yourself.

Our Health and Well-being

Our exploration of health and well-being underscores the importance of self-care for mental and physical health. We've delved into the intricate relationship between mental and physical well-being, the impact of stress, the significance of regular exercise, the role of a balanced diet, and the importance of quality sleep.

Taking care of our bodies and minds is not selfish but necessary. By prioritizing self-care, we enhance our overall quality of life, ensuring we have the energy and resilience to pursue our dreams and goals.

A Farewell to Fear, A Welcome to Fearlessness

As we bid farewell to this book, let it be a farewell to fear and a resounding welcome to fearlessness. Fearless femininity is not a destination; it's a journey—one that we've undertaken together. Armed with wisdom, courage, and a tribe of fierce sisters, you are ready to face whatever comes your way.

So, here's to you. Here's to the woman who embraces imperfections, conquers self-doubt, revels in shared experiences, unleashes her power, celebrates sisterhood, dreams big, practices self-care, and crafts her unique success story.

Celebrate your victories for they inspire others. Challenges are detours, not dead ends. Let's navigate them together. Queens support Queens; let's lift each other higher. Your uniqueness is your superpower, Queen!

As you close this book, remember: the journey doesn't end here. It's a continuous exploration, a dance with fearlessness that you lead. The stage is set, and the spotlight is on you. Now, go out there and shine like the radiant, fearless Diva you are.

FEARLESS FEMININITY

A Love Note from the Author

As I pen down this note, my heart is overflowing with gratitude and a profound sense of sisterhood. "Fearless Femininity" has been a labor of love, a tapestry woven with the threads of shared stories, laughter, and empowerment. To each one of you who embarked on this journey with me, thank you from the depths of my soul.

Thank you for being the heartbeat of this book—the driving force that made every word resonate with authenticity. Your presence on these pages, your vulnerability, and your strength have turned this book into a collective celebration of womanhood.

To those who shared their stories, your courage to bare your souls has created a space where others find solace, inspiration, and the courage to embrace their own narratives. Thank you for being the living embodiment of fearless femininity.

To the sisters who laughed, cried, and nodded along with the tales we shared, you are the heartbeat of this sisterhood. Your energy, enthusiasm, and support have turned this book into a community —a sacred space where women can celebrate, uplift, and inspire each other.

Thank you for being part of this fearless tribe, for embracing imperfections, overcoming self-doubt, and championing the power of sisterhood. This book is a testament to the strength that emerges when women come together, lift each other higher, and celebrate their unique journeys.

With Love,

HAYDE MILLER

www.ingramcontent.com/pod-product-compliance
Lightning Source LLC
Chambersburg PA
CBHW051433090426
42737CB00014B/2952